THROUGH THE THUNDERSTORM

A POETRY THROUGH GRIEF

by Haily Correa

Dorrance Publishing Co
585 Alpha Drive
Pittsburgh, PA 15238
Visit our website at www.dorrancebookstore.com

ISBN: 979-8-8852-7311-4
eISBN: 979-8-8852-7445-6

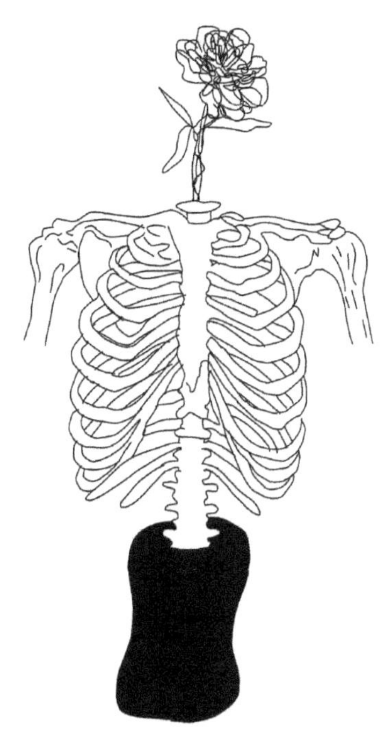

THROUGH THE THUNDERSTORM

A POETRY THROUGH GRIEF

DISTURBANCE

As I lay on the clouds
Listening to the roaring thunderstorm
I ponder whether I should stay or to go
For this place will never be called home

H AILY C ORREA

H E A V Y

I'll water my vase
Until I'm skinny
and pretty
like the roses
that mock me

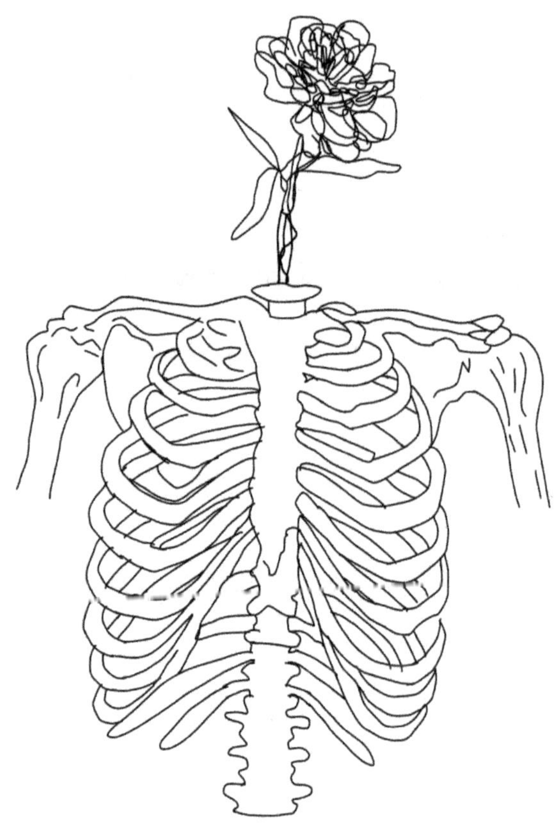

EXHUASTED

My mind races faster than the horses on an open field. Running wild, unattainble, uncontrollable. Running from the storm, to find a safe place to hide. Breath picking up after every step. Mind trying to ease. Panic attacks, not being able to breathe.

FLY TRAP

When you're around my world goes dry, my plants
turn brown, the air becomes virulent. Suffocation.

FIRE

Enlightened empath. The feeling of knowing when someone is lying. That gut wrenching feeling in your chest that makes your heart scorch and fill with anxiety.

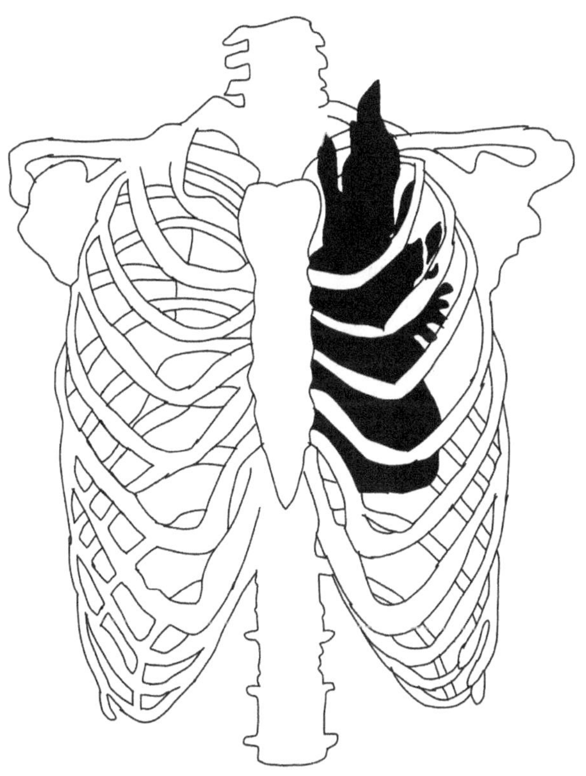

MISSING PIECE

"Votre sourire est un don"
Meaning, your smile is a gift.
The way your hands lock in between mine
The way your lips feel pressed against mine
The way you hold me tight when I want to cry
The way I know that's it hurts not having you by my side

DISCONNECTED

You change like the climate of the weather
making my heart ache
with every twist and turn
I try to follow
just for my heart
to become hollow

REMINISCING

Downhearted is the feeling of seeing their things packed up in boxes. Walking though the empty halls with picture frames off the wall.
The closet being half empty. The bed meant for two now for one.

-The last goodbye.

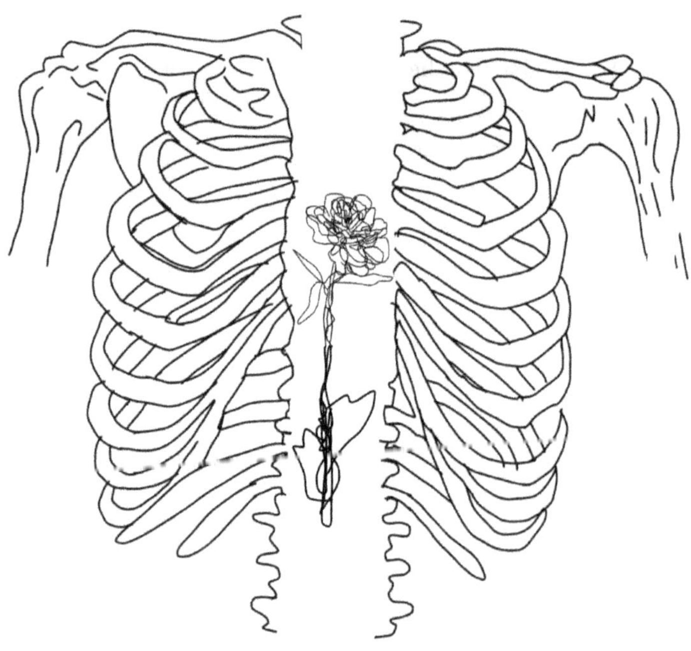

DAMAGE

The way I cared for you, destroyed me into a thousand pieces.

LAST PLACE

I look into the mirror in the deep desire to dissolve and fade away. The trickling tears running down my bare face. I wonder why I am so dissimilar. For you to choose her and not me.

DEMOLISH

Sticks and stones may break my bones, but words shatter my heart, and make my soul frail with withering bones.

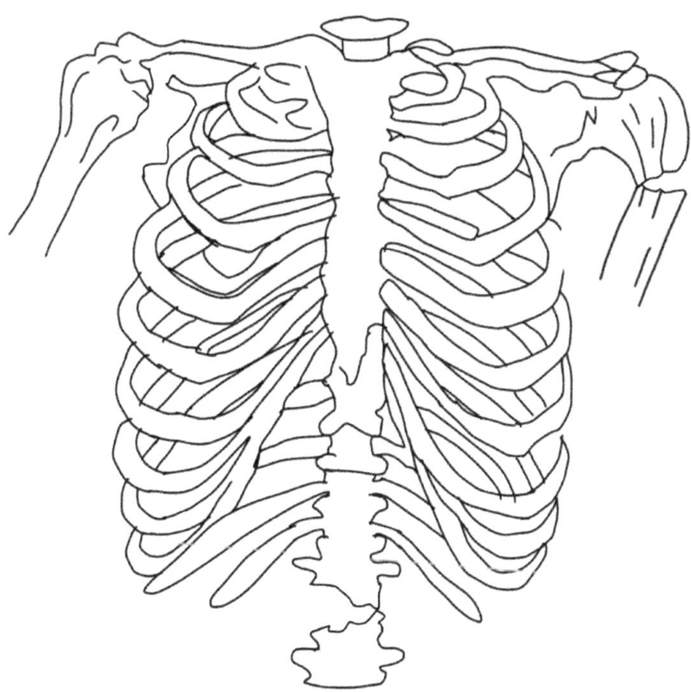

BROKEN CLOCK

Now that we're 21
And no longer 12
You've forgotten of me
And the story we tell
If only you knew
That you were my happily ever after

TEMPORARY

I'm like a dog always loyal and buoying down for my love. They come to me when their lonely but when their happy they stay away. As I am only the comfort and not the home to stay.

Haily Correa

TRYING

The motion of the waves show the pain in your eyes

from the shaky waves
to rocky storm
I know your hurting inside
and I know I am not enough
to cure the past
but I will sure enough
fix the damaged wounds

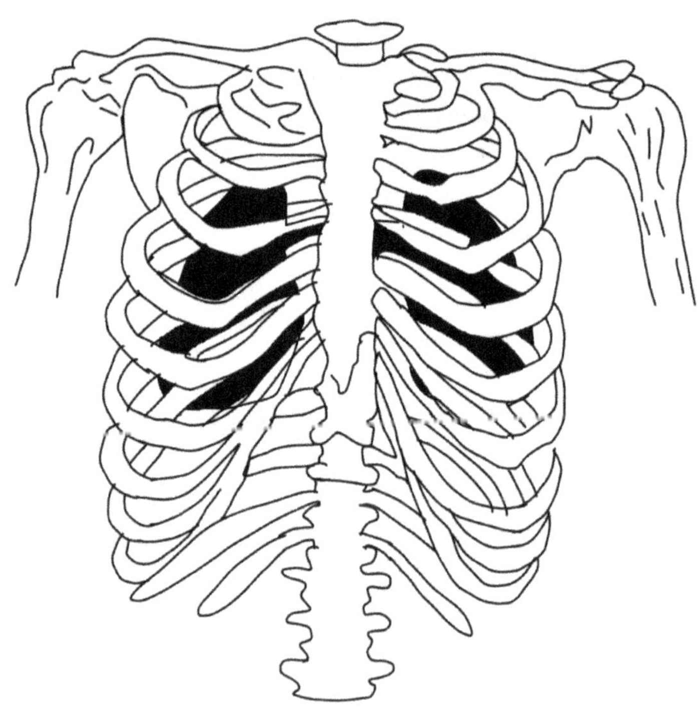

HEALING

When pain comes face to face with you, it seems like it will never leave. But pain is the beginning of beauty.

RECOVERY

Losing you was like broken glass on my skin, the scars still remind me of you, but they are slowing disappearing though my healing.

RISE

I could blame myself and everyone else for losing you. Although blame is not a bandage to my wounds. Picking myself up won't be easy. But sadness can't defeat me.

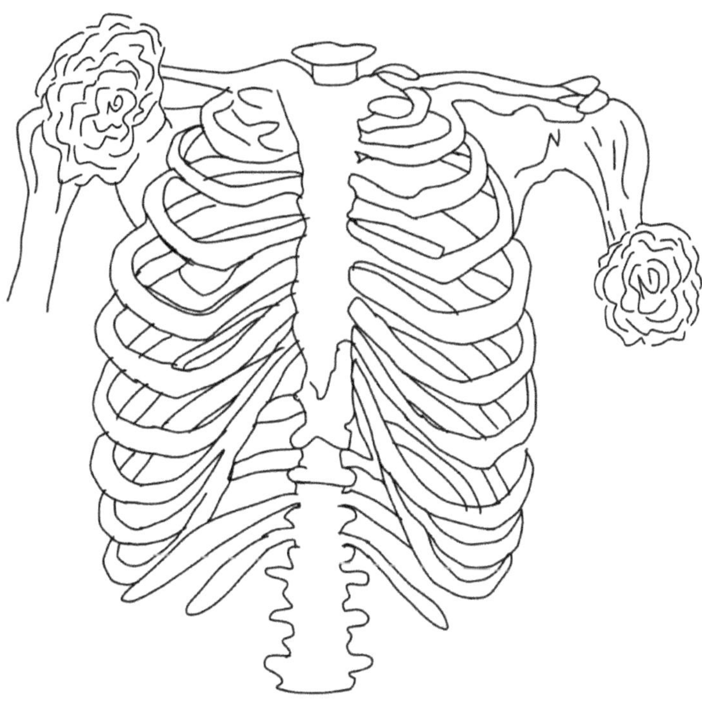

ESTRANGE

I've always tried to hold on to something. Rather it being a dream or desire. But you. I tried to hold you with all my embrace, but all you did was push away.

STALWART

I decided to put myself first, like you did with your little games. I'm tired of my heart being played with, like it's a game of charades. You are just a fool I tried to tame. Now its time for me to be the winner of the game.

REFLECTION

As I map out every detail on your face, pin pointing all my favorite places that you seem to hate. I tell you how all of your so called "flaws" are my favorite type of perfect.

-Mirror

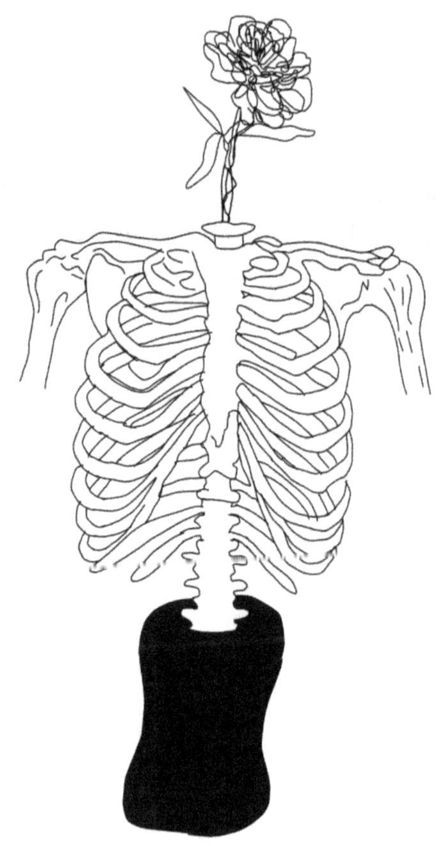

REPLETION

Letting go is hard. Especially when you tried your hardest to hold on. But just like the ocean, you are being filled with toxic oil. And the only way to get better, is by fighting back. Don't hold on to the toxic, instead find the beauty in something good.

CONCEIVABLE

In my head I had a perfect vision of us. We had our suburban home like we always talked about, just out-side the city. Two kids running around the front yard, and a brand new puppy rolling around the grass. But it was just a vision, not a memory.

-What could've been us

INTROSPECTION

As I become the person I want to be, and not a replication of you, I finally began to see true beauty. Being me helps me feel free. But being you feels suffocating.

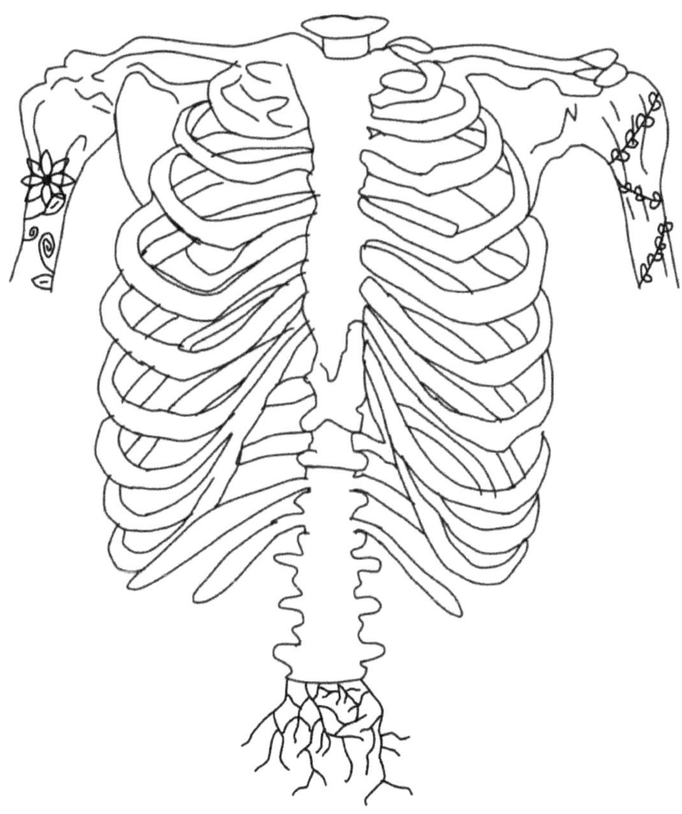

RELEASE

I've tried many ways to detach you from me. I changed my last name, and moved to a city far away. I even pond shopped the ring you gave. But part of me still misses what we had. But letting go physically, is the path to letting go mentally.

INTROSPECTION 2

What I miss most is the person I thought you were. The one who cares about my feelings and doesn't degrade them. The way you used to look at me was my favorite part of the day, but all you did was push away. Why did I let myself believe that you define me, I began to act like you, and like the things you liked, just for you to love me. Why should I degrade myself cause you decided to stop trying. I let you define my beauty, smarts, style, everything. For what? Three words that were always meaningless when they spilled from your lips. Now that I've moved on I've come to realize that I loved a you that you always hid and instead hurt myself with your destruction. Now that your gone I see that you don't define me, I see my beauty, smarts, style, strength all in my vision of being me.

SELFISH

There are people in life that feed off good energy. They find good people that have been hurt but stay strong, make them feel safe and protected in their so called warm embrace. They collect every inch of them. Their heart, brain, skin, secretes, just to abandon them with all the burden and regret. Your existence to them was simply a test to pass or to fail. Leaving you clueless at all that will unveil. For you to pick yourself up again.

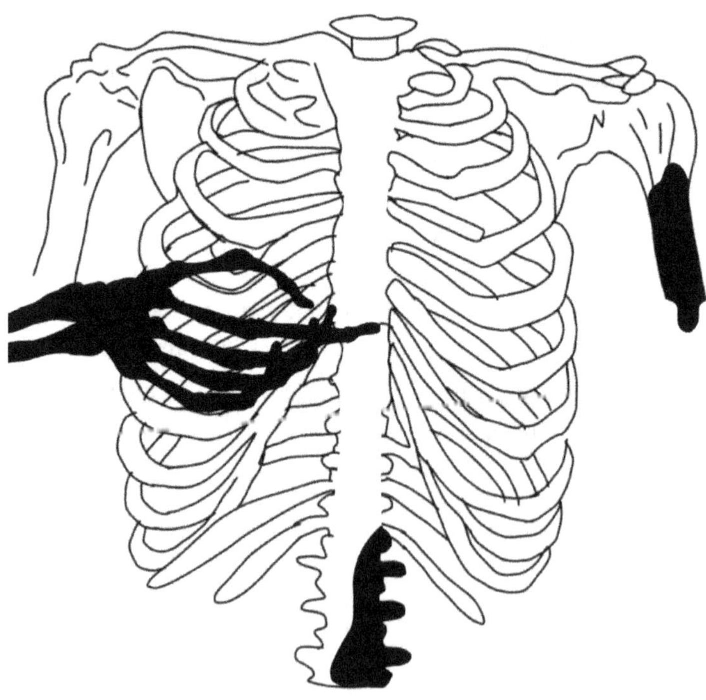

ASSEMBLE

Before starting something new, make sure your mentally okay. You must start a relationship with your self, before you start one with anything else.

- Self-Care

GETTING BETTER

Its hard going through this alone, but what matters is being okay for myself, before being okay for someone else.

RESTORE 1

I am a storm filled with emotions and battle wounds,
I am the fright at the dark clouds but the beauty of
the sun after it rains. I am all I need to become me.

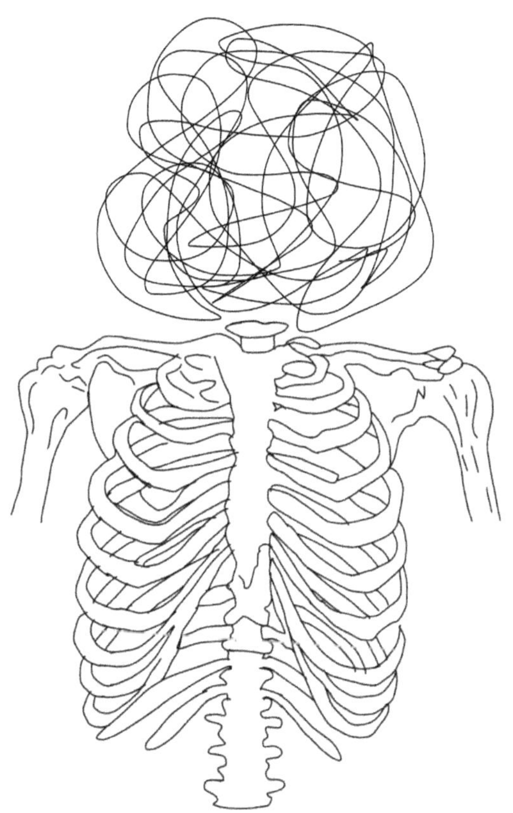

STALKER

Insecurity is a disease that consumes you like mold
on your walls; it caves in, and consumes you until
you are numb. The water from your tears just make
it spread and you try to be bleach perfect blonde,
skinny to bone, and painted perfect like the models
on the wall.

-Insecurity, the disease that always follows.

VALIDATION

Fool, what is a fool exactly? A fool is someone that falls for someone so deeply that they only find that person the brightest star in the sky. They love, care, hold, trust them. They give them everything, their compassion, sorrow, story, truth, life. For what? Betrayal.

-Learning to love yourself first

HEAVY

The color of blue reminds me of you. It's the tears that fall from my face when I think of you. It matches the oceans storms in my heart wishing you had stayed. It matches the skies that are filled with shallowed clouds in my head. Moving on is hard when blue is all around.

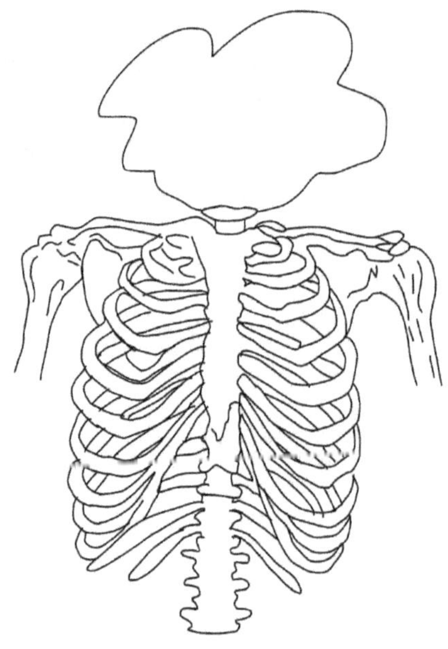

VANISH

As the days wash away, like the tide clears our names, I can't help but think about you, and the impact you made like a strong tidal wave. I miss you like the shells miss the shore, but it's best to pull away, like the waves drag the shells from the sand with our forgotten names.

ELEVATION

You said you loved my long hair, so I cut it short.
You said you loved me brunette, so I went blonde.

You said all these things you loved about me, so I
changed them all so I can finally love me.

BLOOMING

I'm the yellow character. The optimistic, creative, childish, excited over little things. The person that's usually labeled as "annoying" and when calm "boring." But when up for adventure, "too much" or "hyper." I can never be known as what I really am, Unique.

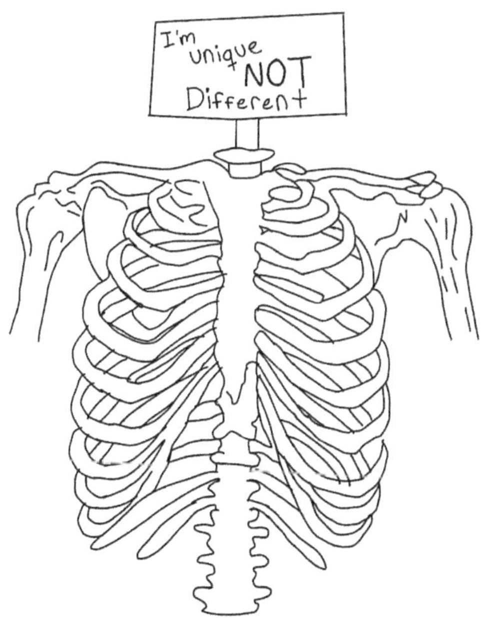

FORTH

I really thought we can manage us, but you wanted to leave us behind as you went forward in life. I wish you could know how empty I feel without you. You hurt me, betrayed me, lied to me, left, yet I still love you. Why? Maybe it's 'cause you were my best friend. Rich or poor, famous or secluded, together or apart, I will always love you, even if I move forward without you.

SINKING

I sunk into the deep depths of the light. I am at peace, not just with myself, but with the world that once burdened me.

DESCRIBE

I melt into the sun's skin as if it was my own. Golden and yellow, like honey brown eyes. Brown is beautiful. It's the disguise of the dirt, the trees, her hair, and her beautiful brown eyes.

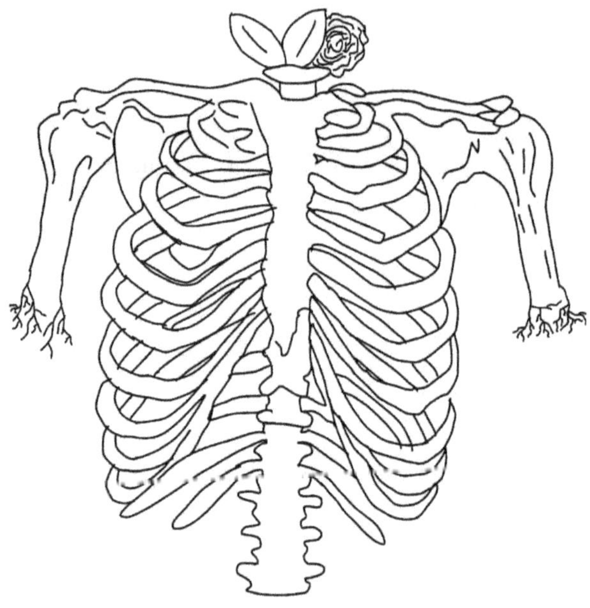

RESTORE 2

I just want someone
To kiss the scars on my skin
And call them beautiful
The battle scars
Of the war
I fought through

VISUALIZE

Nefelibata is a beautiful word meaning
"imagination"
or "cloud walker"
I myself am a cloud walker
wandering in my mind
flooding in my dreams
and desires
Maybe one day
My desirements can come true

TALK

Trauma is something hard to cope with, extremely hard actually. I can write millions or even maybe trillions of pages of all the traumas I've had in my life. There is just one thing; I don't want to fill this book with complete sadness, dejection, or misery. I want to fill this with lessons and emotion. A complete thought if you want to say. Something that someone out there could relate to, that maybe they can understand the sorrow and emptiness. That hopeless feeling in your chest that everything is collapsing. So I can hopefully remind you of your self-worth because believe me, you're so special. You may be muttering something like "you don't know" or "if you knew me you'd hate you," but to be honest hate is a very crucial word. It's a word so dark that most of the time when many people say it they do not mean it. It's partially because you're so angry and built up with emotion the words just slip out. I could never hate someone unless they've done something completely and utterly terrible to me. Something completely unforgivable. Therefore I do not hate you, and yes I do not know you, but what I do know is you're an amazing person and the reason you're reading this book is that you needed some closure or maybe even some comfort, but for whatever reason you're here for, I am so proud of you.

It is not the end of your story.

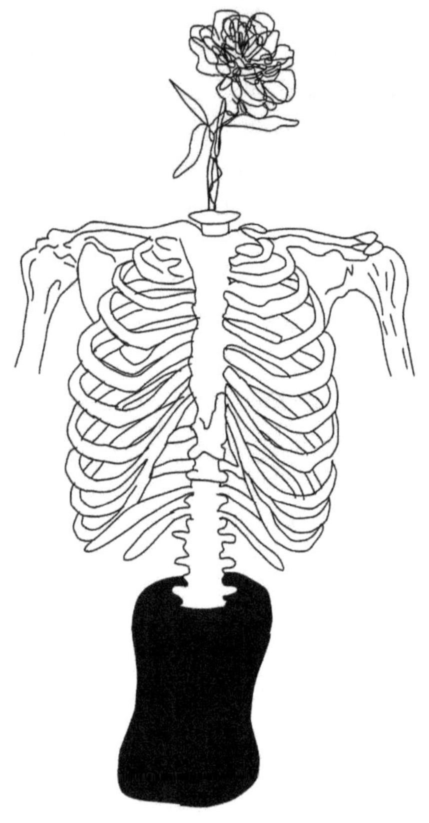